ntents (Third Edition)

The East Berkshire RA Group was formed in 1970 to protect and restore to good order all the public rights of way in this part of Berkshire, and also to seek improvements to the existing footpath network. The Group endeavours to keep under regular surveillance all 1200 paths in the area and will take up irregularities with parish councils, district councils and the County Council to preserve public rights.

Working parties of Group members have cleared over 48 miles of overgrown paths, erected or repaired 605 signposts, built or repaired 220 stiles and 86 footbridges. Regular walks are held, to which newcomers are always welcome, to encourage the use of paths and enjoyment of the countryside. For further details of the Group please contact the Membership Secretary:
Rita North, 14 Gossmore Walk. Gossmore Lane, Marlow, Bucks. SL7 1QZ

Maps in this book are based upon the Ordnance Survey map with the permission of the Controller of H.M. Stationery Office. © Crown copyright.

Gillsmithers Wood and Drawback Hill

This circular walk, after leaving the southern outskirts of Henley-on-Thames, passes through pleasant woods and farmland in and around the attractive Harpsden Valley. The length of the walk is increased to 7 miles when starting from the car park in Mill Lane, or to 8 miles if starting from Henley Railway Station.

Distance: 5¹/₂, 7 or 8 miles
OS Map: Pathfinder 1156 'Henley-on-Thames' and 1172 'Reading'
Start: Henley Station (Grid ref: 763823) but see map for alternatives.

Leaving Station entrance, turn right down Station Road to reach River Thames at Hobbs boat-yard, then turn right along surfaced towpath for about ³/₄ mile to near end of long wooden footbridge leading to Marsh Lock, here turn right up narrow road (Mill Lane). After car park (Grid ref: 771817) on right, pass over railway bridge and with great care cross main road (A4155) into Waterman's Road opposite. Shortly pass through concrete posts and continue up tree-lined bridleway with houses on right. At road junction, continue ahead up Peppard Lane, passing several road-ends on right. Eventually, where tarmac finishes (by No. 36 Cilgerran House), continue ahead along hedged bridleway with field on left.

At end of houses on right, bear slightly right into broad fenced path and shortly keep straight on along road (Greys Road) using footway on right. At entrance to Highlands Farm on left turn left along Highlands Lane and after two pairs of cottages on right, turn right along broad grass strip. Cross field ahead to stile and gap in hedge just to left of trees. Turn half left through middle of next field in direction of distant masts. At solitary tree in middle of field, ignore right fork to reach gap in far boundary, here continue along edge of field ahead with wire fence on left. After stiles either side

of tarmac lane, keep straight on throug middle of field and after stile next to metal gate, continue down through middle of next field to stile on road. Now turn right along road for about 30 yards, then turn sharp left up woodland path through Gillsmithers Wood.

After passing North Lodge to Crowsley Park, keep straight on with park on right, then where metal railings on right bend right, bear left down woodland path. After bottom of hollow ignore crossing track and left fork to continue climbing slightly sunken path, then on emerging from woodland bear right to follow sunken path (Bones Lane) along right-hand edge of field. On reaching 'The Bottle & Glass', with care turn left along road for about ¹/₄ mile to near corner of High Wood on right, here turn right for about 30 yards then after metal gate bear left on broad path through middle of wood.

Emerging on far side of woods, keep straight on along gravel track for about 60 yards and after stile on left, continue along edge of field with fence on right. Do not pass over stile ahead, but turn left along edge of same field to another stile, here continue along edge of next field with fence still on right. After further stile keep straight on through middle of golf course past two white stakes and down gravel track. At corner of wood on right, bear left across grass to pass to left of green, then turn left and descend steps to reach road, here turn right. Shortly at junction, turn right through Harpsden village and immediately after last house on left, turn left into fenced path, and after stile, continue along field edge with fence on left, up Drawback Hill.

Shortly after stile at top of climb, pass across end of road (Rotherfield Road) to enter narrow fenced path ahead. At end of this path, turn right along road for about 100 yards - here is the choice of return route.

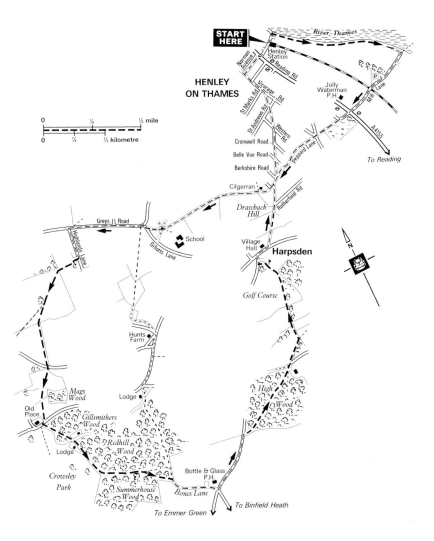

START HERE

River Thames

Norman Avenue

Henley Station

Reading Rd

HENLEY ON THAMES

St Marks Rd

Vicarage Rd

St Andrews Rd

Western Rd

Cromwell Road

Belle Vue Road

Berkshire Road

Cilgerran

Peppard Lane

Jolly Waterman P.H.

Mill Lane

P

A4155

To Reading

Drawback Hill

Rotherfield Rd

0   ¼   ½ mile

0   ¼   ½ kilometre

Greys | Road

Highlands Lane

Gillotts Lane

School

Village Hall

Harpsden

N

Golf Course

Hunts Farm

Mags Wood

Old Place

Gillsmithers Wood

Lodge

Lodge

Redhill Wood

High Wood

Crowsley Park

Summerhouse Wood

Bottle & Glass P.H.

Bones Lane

To Binfield Heath

To Emmer Green

For those going to Mill Lane continue down Peppard Lane; for those going to Station fork left into narrow fenced tarmac path between houses. Keep straight on when path joins road (Cromwell Road), then at junction (Western Road) go left about 15 yards into two more fenced sections of path, and on joining road (Vicarage Road) by pillar box, turn left along road. When road bends left, keep straight on into fenced path to end of school on left, then turn right down broad gravel track and across main road (A4155) to return to Station at start.

DATE WALKED [   ] [19]

Half-way house! 'The Bottle & Glass'

Rotherfield Greys and Stony Bottom

This circular walk, to the north of Sonning Common, is through an open landscape under intensive cultivation and provides extensive views of the Chiltern Hills.

Distance: 4½ miles
OS Map: Pathfinder 1156 'Henley-on-Thames'
Start: Lay-by on Peppard Road (B481) opposite St Michael's Church, Sonning Common (Grid ref: 708807)

Facing the Catholic Church, turn left along road (B481) and at cross-roads at end of bungalows, turn left up Widmore Lane, then after Widmore Pond on right, turn right along Blountscourt Road for about 1/4 mile. About 200 yards after Blounts Farm, turn left over stile to reach near end of hedge, then maintain same direction diagonally through middle of very large field to left-hand end of woodland on right. In next field, continue down edge and keep right through copse in bottom of valley to climb steeply up path ahead with hedge and field on right. Enter field near top of climb and continue with hedge on right.

Just before end of field, pass through hedge on right to cross stile ahead into fenced path leading to lane at red brick house. Now turn left along lane (Kings Farm Lane) and shortly at left-hand bend, keep to right of pair of red brick cottages over stile next to gate. After about 40 yards along track, turn left through gap in hedge, cross stile and follow fence on left to stile and then straight on between paddocks to opening in tree-lined field boundary. Continue straight ahead soon on field edge path to reach Cowfields Farm. Go on, through two wooden field-gates, with section of shingle drive between. At old water trough just ahead turn half left through middle of field to gap in hedge at road junction, here keep straight on along road ahead to Rotherfield Greys.

Arriving in hamlet, note on left - Pear Tree Cottages, built about 1500 and restored in 1947 by the Henley Housing Trust and again in 1985. On right is the building erected by Sir Francis and Lady Stapleton in Commemoration of the Queen's Diamond Jubilee 1897, which in the past has served as both well and bus stop. Immediately after the attractive part 17th Century flint-faced church of St Nicholas, turn left into narrow path along edge of churchyard and after stile ahead, go half right through middle of two fields to reach track after a third stile. Now turn left along track and after wooden swing gate, turn right down gravel track (Dog Lane), then near end of woodland on left, turn left through metal gate into path along edge of woodland.

After about 200 yards, at path junction, turn right over stile through middle of large field. After passing to left of solitary tree on horizon bear left to cross stile on far side, then keep along fenced path with paddock on each side. After high stile by 'Rectory Cottage', turn right along hedged track to reach the Parish Church of All Saints, Rotherfield Peppard (largely rebuilt around 1875) on right. Immediately before the first house on left, turn left into narrow fenced path, then after stile at end and keeping hedge on right, descend steeply into Stony Bottom.

After stile, enter narrow fenced path across valley bottom, then fork slightly left up well-defined track passing Sedgehill Spring on right. At top of climb continue straight on through middle of field, turn right along road for about 150 yards before turning left (by Pineapple Place) into narrow fenced stepped path down to road, here turn left to return to start.

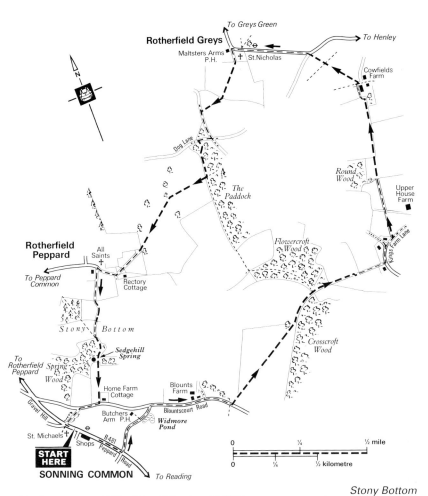

To Greys Green

Rotherfield Greys

Maltsters Arms P.H.

St. Nicholas

To Henley

Cowfields Farm

Dog Lane

The Paddock

Round Wood

Upper House Farm

Rotherfield Peppard

All Saints

To Peppard Common

Rectory Cottage

Flowercroft Wood

Kings Farm Lane

S t o n y   B o t t o m

Sedgehill Spring

Spring Wood

To Rotherfield Peppard

Home Farm Cottage

Butchers Arm P.H.

Blounts Farm

Blountscourt Road

Crosscroft Wood

Widmore Pond

Gravel Hill

St. Michaels

START HERE

SONNING COMMON

Shops

B 481

Peppard Road

To Reading

0	¼	½ mile
0	¼	½ kilometre

Stony Bottom

Chapman's Farm and Chalkhouse Green

This circular walk, on the very outskirts of Reading, is through pleasant gently undulating Chiltern countryside with good views over the surrounding area. In winter and after wet weather, a few places on this walk can be rather muddy, so do go suitably shod.

Distance: 5½ miles
OS Map: Pathfinder 1172 'Reading'
Start: Recreation ground car park, top of Caversham Park Road (Grid ref: 726768)

From car park entrance, turn left along road using broad grass verge on left and directly opposite Northbrook Road, fork left into well-defined tree lined path. Emerging into open, keep straight on with hedge on left and wire mesh fence to School playing field on right to reach track ahead (Foxhill Lane). Turn right along this track for nearly 200 yards, past Littlestead Green Farm on left, then turn left into narrow tarmac lane (Row Lane). About 30 yards along this lane, turn right into firm track along edge of field passing cottages on left to reach road near Dunsden Green. Here turn right along road for about 10 yards, then turn left along edge of field with ditch and wall on right. In far corner of field bear right over footbridge to reach gravel drive of Chapman's Farm.

Cross drive and go straight ahead to stile/footbridge in boundary hedge. Turn left into hedged track (Tagg Lane) gently climbing and curving left, then after house on right keep straight on along gravel drive. Follow left-hand bend at end of drive for only about 30 yards, then turn right over footbridge and through middle of field towards red brick cottage on far side. Shortly pass to right of tree-fringed depression and at bend in field boundary ahead, follow edge of field with hedge on left, to reach road to right of 'The Coach and Horses' ahead. Cross road into gravel drive opposite, pass to left of farm buildings and continue ahead along edge of large field with hedge on right. Follow right-hand

edge of next field, passing two mature oaks, then, with field opening ahead, bear left to continue along field edge still with hedge on right.

At end of field, after red brick cottages on left, turn right along road for nearly half a mile to 'Bird in Hand' at cross-roads, here with care cross B481 into lane opposite. At junction ahead, with care turn left along road (Kennylands Road) keeping to verge on left for just over 100 yards, then turn right over stile and through middle of large field in direction of distant buildings. At far side, cross stile and follow field edge with wire fence on left. Cross stiles either side of small field ahead then bear left alongside fence. After further stile go along gravel drive to reach road at Chalkhouse Green.

Now turn left and at end of tarmac road enter hedged track (Chalkhousegreen Lane), then follow this winding undulating bridleway for about ¾ mile. On reaching road (B481), with care cross over and turn right along verge for about 30 yards, then turn left into Tower Close passing Emmer Green Tower on right. Pass to left of No. 15 into Marchwood Avenue ahead, turn right for about 40 yards, then turn left into fenced path to right of No. 12 and at end of tarmac path, turn right into narrow hedged path with two stiles. At road ahead (Kiln Road), turn left for just over 100 yards past Reservoir on right, then turn right into gravel track (Foxhill Lane) which continues along left-hand side of Blackhouse Wood ahead. Immediately after woodland, turn right along track to retrace route used at beginning and to return to car park at start.

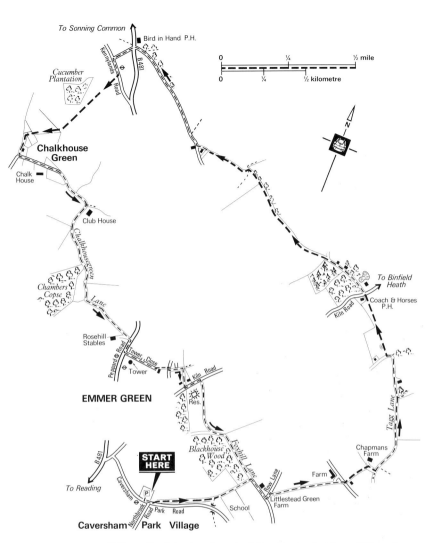

To Sonning Common

Bird in Hand P.H.

Cucumber Plantation

Kennylands Road
B481

Chalkhouse Green

Chalk House

Club House

Chambers Copse

Chalkhousegreen Lane

Rosehill Stables

Peppard Road

Tower Close

Tower

EMMER GREEN

Res.

Blackhouse Wood

Kiln Road

To Binfield Heath

Coach & Horses P.H.

Kiln Road

Tagg Lane

Chapmans Farm

Foxhill Lane

Row Lane

Farm

Littlestead Green Farm

START HERE

B481

To Reading

Caversham Road

Northbrook Road

Park Road

School

Caversham Park Village

0   ¼   ½ mile
0   ¼   ½ kilometre

N

Chiltern Society members building the footbridge off Tagg Lane

Highland Wood and Walk Shaw

This mostly flat circular walk is through typical Chiltern countryside.

Distance: 4 miles
OS Map: Pathfinder 1172 'Reading'
Start: Limited verge parking in lane on east side of 'The Fox Inn', Cane End (Grid ref: 680795). For patrons, 'The Pack Horse' on A4074 (Grid ref: 692781) is an alternative.

With your back to main road (A4074) and 'The Fox Inn' on left, go ahead along small lane and shortly at cross-roads, turn right along road keeping to verge on right. Immediately after second property 'Owlswood' on right, enter field on right through gap in hedge, then go half left through middle of field, aiming for gap to right of tall trees in far boundary. Maintain same direction through middle of next field to row of seven trees - aiming for right-hand side of second tree from left. At tree, turn half left to reach stile in hedge at road just beyond double power line pole. Now turn right along road to bend, here before property 'Ashfield', turn right into hedged and fenced path to eventually enter woodland - Highland Wood.

Keep straight on through woodland following waymarks (painted white arrows) with fields nearby on left, then where boundary bends right continue with fence on left. On reaching main road (A4074) ahead climb up bank and with extreme care turn left along road, keeping to verge on left - there is a parallel route below on left, but at time of writing the landowner was not prepared to grant formal access. At top of climb (Green Dean Hill) and within sight of 'The Pack Horse' with care turn right across road into lane opposite. Follow lane through left-hand bend, then immediately after cottages on right at Tinkers Green, turn right into tarmac track and shortly continue along hedged path. Follow this path through right and left-hand bends to eventually reach the buildings of Hodmore Farm, here in front of red brick cottage, turn left between buildings and along concrete farm road. At road ahead, turn right along road keeping to right-hand side (to face oncoming traffic) and immediately before large property 'Cross Lanes' on right, turn right into hedged path. At bottom of descent follow path through left-hand bend, then slowly climb to eventually reach junction of paths at bend in field boundary on left, here turn right along wide track, following low bank of wooded Walk Shaw on left.

Where path narrows, continue ahead until, emerging from woodland, bear right along edge of field for about 20 yards, then turn left through metal swing gate and follow edge of field with fence on left. Near end of field pass over stile (next to metal gate) on left and continue with fence on left. Shortly at tennis court ahead, turn right and after stile next to large metal gate, with care cross road to return to start.

DATE WALKED   19

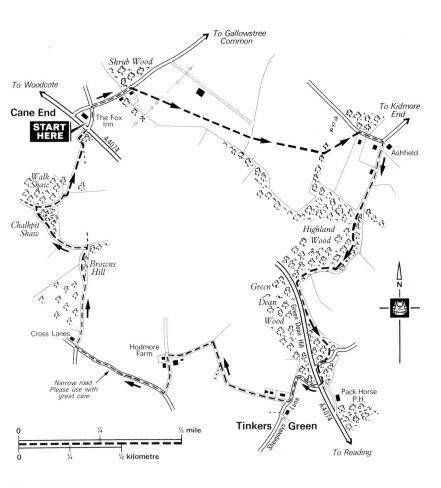

To Gallowstree Common

Shrub Wood

To Woodcote

Cane End

START HERE

The Fox Inn

A4074

To Kidmore End

Ashfield

Walk Shaw

Chalkpit Shaw

Browns Hill

Highland Wood

Green Dean Wood

Green Dean Hill

Cross Lanes

Hodmore Farm

Narrow road Please use with great care.

N

Pack Horse P.H.

Tinkers Green

Sheepways Lane

A4074

To Reading

| 0 | ¼ | ½ mile |

| 0 | ¼ | ½ kilometre |

Near Walk Shaw

Nuney Green and Path Hill

Ramble 5

This circular walk, through sparsely populated countryside to the north-west of Reading, is for most of the route either through, or within sight of beautiful beech woodland.

Distance: 4 miles
OS Map: Pathfinder 1172 'Reading'
Start: Opposite 'King Charles
            Head' (limited verge parking)
            (Grid ref: 664788)

Facing the 'King Charles Head', turn left along verge for about 150 yards, then turn sharp right into winding waymarked (painted white arrows) well-defined path for about half a mile through Gutteridge's Wood. On reaching narrow tarmac road, opposite white thatched cottage, fork left along road to junction, by property 'Cross Ways' at Nuney Green.

Now turn left along gravel track, then keep straight on into hedged path between thatched properties to enter woodland ahead and shortly to follow edge of wood with long narrow field nearby on right. Continue 15 yards beyond path junction, at near corner of large field on right, fork half left along waymarked woodland path for about 150 yards, then fork right into a narrower waymarked woodland path with earth bank nearby on left. On reaching field on left, continue along edge of woods and at brick bungalow on left cross over road (Deadman's Lane) into fenced path opposite.

After stile ahead follow fence on left to pass through swing-gate and turn right, now with fence on right. Pass through another swing-gate and bear left across end of field between hawthorn and beech hedges. Leave field over stile and enter hedged path ahead. On far side of buildings, immediately turn left past Alnutt's Hospital - in his will in 1724, Henry Alnutt left his estate to the benefit of the ten almshouses and chapel (with clock tower over) surrounding this cobbled courtyard. At entrance to

'Chaplaincy', fork right along broad grass (permitted) path to reach, after wooden swing gate, road junction at Goring Heath.

Pass to right of Post Office opposite to enter, through wooden swing gate, tree-lined path, then at end of field on right, turn right into very narrow fenced path* with hedge on left. At stile ahead, the correct line of the path turns half-left across field towards left-hand of two distant cottages, to reach stile to right of metal gate. Cross track (Bunces Lane) to pass between cottages opposite. Shortly after farm gate, enter field on right to pass to right of copse ahead. At stile in corner of field, continue straight on down edge of field and after two more stiles, either side of steep valley, continue through woodland ahead to soon reach narrow lane at Path Hill, here turn left along lane.

Pass to left of Path Hill Farm and about 120 yards into woodland ahead along well defined firm track, in bottom of small depression, turn left down woodland track. At bottom of valley, by field exit on left, bear right, up straight climbing waymarked woodland path. On arriving at edge of woods, do not take stile ahead to white cottage, but turn left over another stile and up edge of field with hedge on right, to reach after small metal gate, road at Collins End Common. Now turn left along road and about 80 yards after 'Briar Cottage' on right, turn right along fenced track, then where this bends right, pass through stileway into field ahead. Continue with hedge on right and after two more stiles, go through middle of small paddock and stile in hedge to return to start.

This recently fenced path is too narrow. It is the Highway Authority's responsibility to receive complaints and take the appropriate action. Be very careful not to tear your clothes.

DATE WALKED | | 19

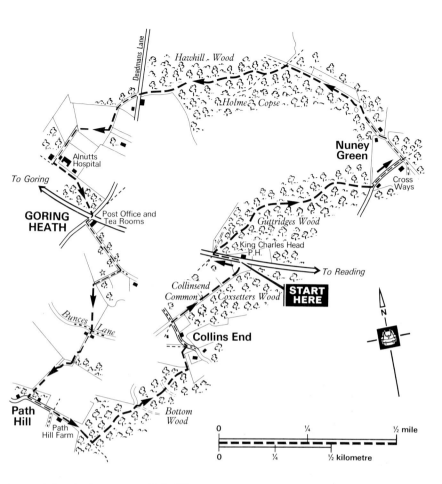

Long winter shadows across Path Hill

Whitchurch Hill and Boze Down

This circular walk, to the north of Pangbourne, after climbing up through Whitchurch to Whitchurch Hill, passes through green pastures and cultivated farmland with some good views across the Thames Valley.

Distance: 5 miles
OS Map: Pathfinder 1172 'Reading'
Start: Small car park (free on Sundays) Pangbourne side of Whitchurch toll-bridge (Grid ref: 636767)

From car park, turn right over toll-bridge (pedestrians free), then turn left into Private Drive (a public path) towards The Mill and after about 80 yards turn right into narrow walled path leading to the attractive flint-faced Parish Church of St Mary the Virgin. At lych-gate bear right along gravel track to rejoin road, here turn left up through the picturesque village of Whitchurch. At top of village, bear left along narrower road, then shortly make use of the full length of raised verge on right before crossing road to War Memorial opposite.

Keep along verge for about another 50 yards, then fork left up broad path to cross stile ahead and follow edge of field with hedge on left. At end of field, go through metal swing-gate into fenced grass track ahead. Pass to right of Beech Farm buildings and cross concrete drive to enter field by swing-gate and follow fence on left. DO NOT leave field through gate ahead but instead turn right along edge of field and after another swing gate, rejoin and continue along concrete drive. With care cross over road (B471) ahead and turn right past the Church of St John the Baptist, Whitchurch Hill.

At end of churchyard, fork left across middle of Green, to enter to right of houses ahead, a fenced path. After metal swing gate, bear left through middle of fields (towards left-hand end of row of trees on horizon) to reach another swing gate, here turn right along

fenced farm track. After stile into field ahead, keep along edge of field with fence on left and in next field (at path junction) bear right around edge of field with fence on right to stile in corner, here turn left up track for about 60 yards then turn right over stile and along edge of field with hedge on left. After 'squeeze' stile at corner of field, keep along gravel drive, turn left along road past Path Hill House on left, then where road bends left, go right along winding lane. Immediately before Path Hill Farm ahead, turn right into private road (a public path) and at end of drive, enter by stile, steeply descending hedged path. After stiles at either side of road ahead, continue ahead along edge of field with hedge on left towards Boze Down.

In corner of field, pass through metal swing gate. On entering field ahead, turn left down edge with hedge on left and after swing gate at bottom, turn right along road keeping to verge on right. After Boze Down Vineyard*, keep to the Jubilee (Queen's Silver 1977) Walk - the raised verge on right - then about 100 yards after 'Whitchurch-on-Thames' sign, turn left down small steps and across road to enter broad gravel track with allotments on left. At end of Cricket Ground on right, turn right along road, Eastfield Lane, to reach village by 'The Greyhound', here turn left to cross the River Thames again, to return to car park at start.

Free tastings every weekend in the shop! (Open 11am-6pm Sat, noon-5pm Sun)

DATE WALKED [   ][19]

Boze Down

Pangbourne College and River Pang

This circular walk, to the west and south of Pangbourne, follows the River Thames for nearly a mile, then after climbing up to Pangbourne College, descends through cultivated fields to Tidmarsh before returning along the banks of the River Pang.

Distance: 5 miles
OS Map: Pathfinder 1172 'Reading'
Start: Car park in centre of Pangbourne, next to 'Copper Inn' (Grid ref: 634765)

From car park, turn left along road and under railway arch. Continue along Shooters Hill (A329) to eventually keep to footway on right with River Thames nearby. Where river starts to curve away from road, by bus stop, turn left across road to pass under railway, then immediately take left fork into climbing, winding woodland path, crossing stile a little way up.

After another stile, near top of climb, continue straight on through scattered beech woodland, Berry's Copse, then after emerging by metal swing gate, bear left along edge of field with metal fence on left. After another swing gate at end of field, maintain same direction through middle of next field, towards left-hand end of copse on right. At corner of copse enter next field, to bear left along grass path with hedge on left. At end of field, pass through metal swing gate and with care turn left along road, then at junction, bear slightly right into narrow lane opposite, leading to Pangbourne College - founded by Sir Thomas Lane Devitt and his son Philip in 1917 to educate and train boys for the Royal and Merchant Navies.

Go ahead, passing tennis courts on right and at crossing tarmac drive, turn left to pass new 1991 College building on right. Shortly turn sharp right then bear left into gently descending gravel track passing cottage ('Rivendell') on left. After crossing road (Bere Court Road) ahead, continue down gravel drive opposite and at isolated house 'Spindleberry' on right, enter hedged path and follow this through left-hand bend. At end of long sunken field on right, turn right across end of this field with hedge on left and follow this grassy track through left-hand bend along right-hand side of next field.

Near end of field, follow track through right-hand bend and up slope, then after stile next to metal gate, continue down edge of next small field, with fence on right, to reach road after small wooden swing gate. Now turn left down road and at junction ahead, opposite 'The Greyhound' turn left along road (The Street, A340) then at end of footway on left, turn right across road, pass through swing-gate and along fenced path, soon within sight of the Pang.

Follow this fenced path, noting its 'permitted' status* as it skirts round a pretty riverside cottage - 'Longbridge'. On reaching entrance to this property, turn left along tree-lined tarmac drive. Keep straight on along gravel track then at metal field gate ahead, turn right over stile and along right-hand side of field to reach, after another stile, the west bank of the River Pang. On reaching concrete footbridge, turn right over river and after stile, turn left to follow other bank, then where river bends left, keep straight on to enter fenced path ahead through wooden swing gate. Eventually continue along gravel road, The Moors, between houses and at Reading Road ahead, turn left to return to car park at start.

*At time of publication this section of path had not been officially diverted from its original route straight ahead, alongside cottage.

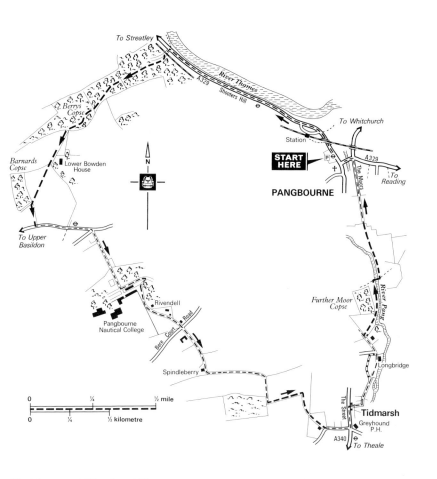

To Streatley

River Thames

A 329

Shooters Hill

To Whitchurch

Station

Berrys Copse

Barnards Copse

Lower Bowden House

N

START HERE

A 329

PANGBOURNE

The Moors

To Reading

To Upper Basildon

Rivendell

Further Moor Copse

River Pang

Pangbourne Nautical College

Bere Court Road

Spindleberry

Longbridge

The Street

Tidmarsh

Greyhound P.H.

A 340

To Theale

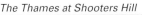

| 0 | ¼ | ½ mile |
| 0 | ¼ | ½ kilometre |

The Thames at Shooters Hill

Moor Copse and Sulham Woods

Ramble 8

This circular walk, immediately to the west of Reading, is through the rich agricultural land around Sulham and provides some fine views over the valley of the River Pang. The walk is almost entirely within the North Wessex Downs Area of Outstanding Natural Beauty.

Distance: 3¼ miles
OS Map: Pathfinder 1172 'Reading'
Start: Small parking area at entrance to Sulham Woods (Grid ref: 648745)

With your back to road, enter Sulham Woods through stileway to follow the left-hand woodland path and shortly at clearing, bear right for about 60 yards, then bear left down winding woodland path. Emerging from woodland by stile, follow edge of field ahead with fence on left and at end of the field on left, turn left over stile into fenced path with properties below on right. After stile at entrance to field, continue straight on with hedge on left to reach road, here cross over if you wish to visit the small but impressive church of St Nicholas, Sulham - built in 1832, it replaced one that had stood on or near this site since the late 13th century.

To continue walk, turn right down road and about 40 yards after road junction, pass over stile on left and bear right through middle of field. After two stiles at footbridge, maintain same direction through next field and after stile in far corner, continue along edge of next field to follow on right, stream and Moor Copse.

On reaching footbridge on right, turn left for about 50 yards, then turn right over stile and along field edge with woodland (Horsemoor Wood) on right. At end of this long field, turn left along edge of field (headland) with bank and trees on right - the red brick tower in distance on right is the remains of a folly. The farmer prefers people to use this headland rather than the official path running parallel on the other side of the

bank, so it is hoped he will soon apply for an official diversion. On reaching gravel farm track (Nunhide Lane) at far side of field, here move to the right a few paces then continue ahead up edge of next field with hedge on left, to reach again the Forestry Commission's Sulham Woods.

Now take care to turn right for about 30 yards before entering woodland, then continue steeply up narrow climbing woodland path. Emerging from woodland by stile, keep straight on with fence and then hedge on left to reach road (Little Heath Road) after stile, here opposite school, turn left along road for nearly ½ mile. Where road bends right, opposite property No. 27, turn left over stile and along edge of field with fence on right, then at end of field on right, turn half left on well-defined path through middle of large field. Just after pond by remains of Sadler's Farm, turn right along mid-field track to reach, after stile, parking place at start.

DATE WALKED   19

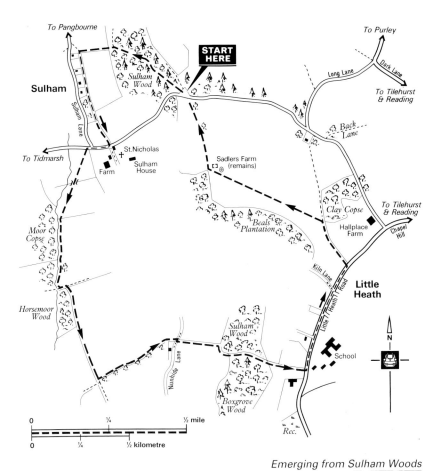

Sulham

To Pangbourne

Sulham Wood

START HERE

To Purley

Dark Lane

Long Lane

To Tilehurst & Reading

Back Lane

Sulham Lane

To Tidmarsh

St. Nicholas

Farm

Sulham House

Sadlers Farm (remains)

Clay Copse

Hallplace Farm

To Tilehurst & Reading

Chapel Hill

Moor Copse

Beals Plantation

Kiln Lane

Little Heath

Horsemoor Wood

Sulham Wood

Nunhide Lane

School

Boxgrove Wood

Little Heath Road

N

Rec.

0   ¼   ½ mile

0   ¼   ½ kilometre

Emerging from Sulham Woods

North Street and Englefield Estate

This flat circular walk is to the west of Theale, a village restored to tranquillity by the construction of the M4. Our route is over farmland and along quiet lanes, forming part of the Englefield Estate, one of the largest private estates.

Distance: 4 miles
OS map: Pathfinder 1172 'Reading'
Start: Car park (free on Sundays) at east end of Theale High St (Grid ref: 646715)

Leaving car park, turn left along road and at end of houses on left, turn left over stile into fenced and hedged path. After crossing bridge over stream, turn left along edge of field with trees and housing on left to remains of metal fence, then continue straight on through middle of next field to reach road (Blossom Lane), here turn right along road. At end of tarmac lane, turn left past 'Blossomsend Cottage' and through metal farm gate, to enter and follow through right-hand bend, broad hedged grass path. After stile next to wooden field gate, bear slightly left through middle of field to footbridge over ditch, then continue slightly left, passing large solitary oak on right, to reach another stile, here turn right along fenced path. The spire of Englefield Church, to be visited later, may be seen in the distance on left. At road ahead, turn right along road to pass through the hamlet of North Street.

About 50 yards after last house (The Grange) on left, turn left over stile through middle of field keeping parallel at first with boundary on left. On meeting field boundary, continue with ditch and hedge on left to reach road after stile, here turn left along road. On reaching junction with main road (A340), with care cross over and continue ahead along road (The Street) through Englefield - a picturesque village entirely in the ownership of the Englefield Estate.

At far end of village, turn right up drive past the Deer Park on left, to visit the impressive flint-faced Parish Church of St Mark's - it's earliest part is the Nave dating from 1190. Further up, among the trees on left, is Englefield House - a magnificent Elizabethan mansion (yes, SHE dined here in September 1601), home of the Benyon family for some 250 years. The 7-acre gardens are open to the public every Monday. Englefield Village is owned by the estate which covers some 14,000 acres comprising a Home Farm of 2,000 acres, 23 'let' farms and 3,000 acres of woodland. There is unrestricted public access to most of the woodland including Pamber Forest, an SSSI of ancient oak woodland, managed as a Nature Reserve.

Now retrace your steps through the village, then immediately before the last house on right, turn right through metal swing gate into fenced path and after stile continue straight on through middle of field. After footbridge over ditch bear slightly left through middle of next field to reach main road (A340) after stile, opposite Wickcroft Farm, here with care turn right along road keeping to verge on right. At gatehouse to Englefield Park, turn left along Englefield Road and just after side road on left, pass through swing-gate on left to follow right hand edge of playing field before rejoining road at second swing-gate. Within a few yards cross road into Village Hall car park and then over playing field to reach entrance to churchyard, behind childrens' playground. Follow path through churchyard, with the lofty stone Holy Trinity Church on left and at road ahead, turn left along road through Theale to return to car park at start.

DATE WALKED   19

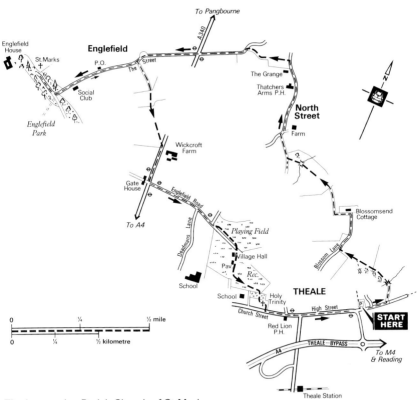

Englefield House
St.Marks
Englefield
Englefield
P.O.
The Street
To Pangbourne
A.340
The Grange
Thatchers Arms P.H.
North Street
Social Club
Farm
Englefield Park
N
Wickcroft Farm
Gate House
Englefield Road
Blossomsend Cottage
To A4
Deadmans Lane
Playing Field
Blossom Lane
Village Hall
Pav
Rec.
THEALE
School
School
Holy Trinity
High Street
Church Street
P
START HERE
Red Lion P.H.
A4
THEALE BYPASS
To M4 & Reading
Theale Station

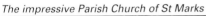

0   ¼   ½ mile
0   ¼   ½ kilometre

The impressive Parish Church of St Marks

Simms Copse and Kiln Pond

Ramble 10

This circular walk passes through the pleasant undulating countryside of fields and woods around Mortimer West End and is entirely in the county of Hampshire.

Distance: 4 miles
OS map: Pathfinder 1188 'Mortimer and Arborfield'
Start: Recreation ground car park off Church Road, Mortimer West End (Grid ref: 634640)

From car park, turn left along Church Road, then immediately opposite Slade Lodge turn left to follow edge of field with hedge on right. After garage, keep on through middle of field and then along farm track, passing buildings of West End Farm close on right. Continue ahead down track, then shortly after turning right under power lines, turn left through first gateway into narrow field. Go ahead through opening and climb up edge of next field with woods on right, then on entering field ahead, maintain same direction to reach stile at road, here turn right along road.

Just over 100 yards after 'Ye Olde Turners Arms' turn right over ditch and follow path along field edge (headland) with hedge on right. (The farmer obviously prefers people to use this headland rather than the official path on the other side of the hedge, so it is hoped he will soon apply for an official diversion.) Keep straight on over two more stiles and along fenced path to reach road (Turks Lane) at Summerlug, here turn right along road then shortly fork right into lane (Simms Farm Lane). At end of tarmac, turn right into gravel drive and after stile behind Rose Cottage, turn left along edge of field with fence on left. After stile ahead, enter valley path through Simms Copse.

Emerging from copse over stile, turn right down field edge with copse on right and after stile, pass over wooden footbridge. Now bear slightly right through middle of field ahead, avoiding corner, then continue along field boundary on right, through this and following field. In far corner of second field cross two stiles with gravel track between and continue in paddock with fence on right. Cross stile by gate and keeping left of hedgerow ahead finally enter woodland path in corner of this field. Shortly at path junction turn left and at top of rise, turn right for about 25 yards to stile at top of bank, then turn half right through middle of field to another stile in middle of woodland. Cross over footbridge in bottom of copse then climb up to road, here with care turn right along road keeping to verge on right. Shortly, at end of copse on left, turn left into and down winding gravel track to reach Kiln Pond.

Cross over the embankment between the two ponds and on far side, continue along track. Where track turns left, continue ahead to right of tall tree and at top of rise turn right. Shortly before field ahead turn left to follow edge of young woodland with field nearby on right. After crossing stream, fork right and climb up to reach road, here turn left along road to return to car park at start.

DATE WALKED | | 19

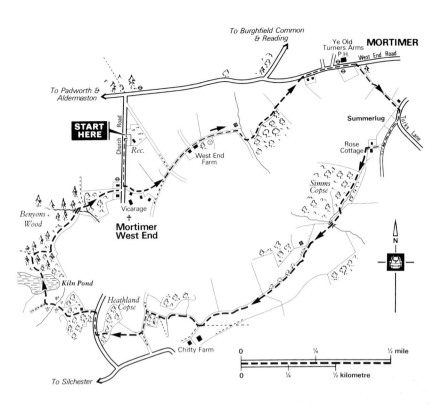

To Burghfield Common & Reading

Ye Old Turners Arms P.H.

MORTIMER

West End Road

To Padworth & Aldermaston

START HERE

Church Road

Rec.

Summerlug

Tuffts Lane

West End Farm

Rose Cottage

N

Vicarage

Mortimer West End

Simms Copse

Benyons Wood

Kiln Pond

Heathland Copse

Chitty Farm

0   ¼   ½ mile

0   ¼   ½ kilometre

To Silchester

Ramblers' Association members at the Foudry Brook footbridge (Ramble 13)

Ufton Court and Seward's Gully

Ramble 11

This circular walk, through a variety of countryside, does a complete circuit of Ufton Nervet and includes some good distant views of the Kennet Valley.

Distance: 4 miles
OS map: Pathfinder 1188 'Mortimer and Arborfield'
Start: Verge parking near crossroads about ¼ mile southwest of Sulhamstead Abbots (Grid ref: 644677)

From cross-roads, go south along Hollybush Lane for nearly half a mile, keeping to verge on right, then opposite light-painted houses turn right along drive towards Benhams Farm. Pass through middle of farm buildings to enter fenced path through wooden swing gate and after a further swing gate, continue ahead on gravel track. After wooden swing gate next to cattle grid, turn right along road (Island Farm Road) for about 125 yards, enter woodland (Poors Allotments) on left. A temporary diversion of the footpath here for gravel extraction purposes with subsequent restoration and tree planting, has been agreed. Please follow waymarked gravel path to eventually reach stile in corner of adjoining field, here continue along edge of field with hedge on left.

In next corner, bear left over stile next to wooden swing gate to pass between cottages and along their gravel drive. Cross over (Camp Road) and continue ahead along broad ride (Church Plantation) to reach road on far side. Bear right for a few yards to road junction, then turn left through gateway and bear right to enter field by stile. Go half right through middle of field to stile (to right of metal field gate) in front of right-hand house on far boundary. Now turn right along edge of grass to shortly see on left the Elizabethan front of Ufton Court. The house, which dates from the late 15th century, was the home of the Perkins family, Catholic recusants who gave sanctuary to many priests in the days of Elizabeth I. Now turn right along tarmac drive between broad avenue of oaks and on reaching the thatched Ufton Court Lodge at road, turn left along road. About 125 yards after end of woodland on right, turn right over stile and through middle of field to another stile, here descend to cross small footbridge over Seward's Gully.

After further stile on far side of gully, continue along edge of field with woodland on left, to shortly see through trees ahead, the tower and spire of St Peter's Church, Ufton Nervet. Pass to left of pond and through middle of field ahead to enter track to left of cream-painted cottage. At road (Church Lane) ahead, turn left for about 20 yards, then turn right over stile to follow edge of two fields, the first with fence on right and the second with row of oaks on left. Emerging from corner of field, with care cross road (Sulhamstead Road) into fenced gravel track opposite and at junction cross into St Michaels Lane ahead. After the buildings of Meales Farm, turn right through metal swing gate into St Michael's Burial ground - all that now remains of the flint-faced Church (built in 1912 and demolished in 1967) is the porch, left as a shelter for funeral mourners.

Leaving far end of burial ground by stile, continue across end of field with fence on right. Do not go over stile ahead, but turn right down edge of large field with fence on left, then after small wooden swing gate at bottom, keep straight on over stream and steeply up woodland path. Near top of climb continue ahead along edge of woodland, then where track turns left, keep straight on to shortly enter the churchyard to the small flint-faced 13th century Church of St Mary's, Sulhamstead Abbots. Emerge from churchyard past the thatched 'Church Cottage' and at junction, turn right along road (Short Heath Lane) to return to start.

DATE WALKED 19

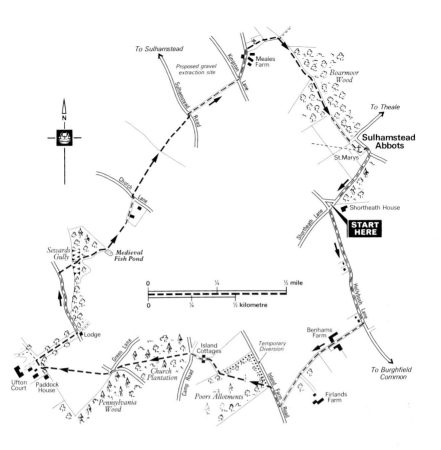

To Sulhamstead

Proposed gravel extraction site

Kingston Lane

Meales Farm

Boarmoor Wood

To Theale

Sulhamstead Abbots

St. Marys

Sulhamstead Road

Church Lane

N

Shortheath House

START HERE

Shortheath Lane

Sewards Gully

Medieval Fish Pond

0   ¼   ½ mile

0   ¼   ½ kilometre

Lodge

Green Lane

Island Cottages

Temporary Diversion

Hollybush Lane

Benhams Farm

Ufton Court

Paddock House

Pennsylvania Wood

Church Plantation

Camp Road

Poors Allotments

Island Farm Road

Firlands Farm

To Burghfield Common

Ufton Court - also visited (via a different route) in the first series

Ufton Green and
Padworth House

This walk follows the restored Kennet and Avon Canal and also provides fine views over the wide Kennet Valley. It is particularly suitable for those using public transport as it can be a linear walk from Theale or Wigmore Lane, or a circular walk from Aldermaston. For motorists, a new car park at Tyle Mill Bridge provides another starting point.

Distance: Linear: 4 miles (Wigmore Lane) or 5½ miles (Theale). Circular: 6 miles
           (plus 2 miles if starting from Wigmore Lane)

OS map: Pathfinder 1188 'Mortimer and Arborfield'

❶ From THEALE STATION - turn left along road and at far side of swing bridge over canal, turn right along towpath for just over 1½ miles to reach Tyle Mill Bridge.

❷ From BUS STOP ON A4 - go to south end of Wigmore Lane, cross railway, turn right to first power pole and then turn left through copse. Shortly, after footbridge, turn right along bank of River Kennet, turn left over footbridge, cross swing bridge ahead and turn right along towpath for about ½ mile to reach Tyle Mill Bridge.

❸ From ALDERMASTON - start from the north side of the Kennet and Avon Canal at Aldermaston (Grid ref: 602672), at the plaque unveiled on 11th September 1986 to mark the completion of the restoration of Aldermaston Lock and Wharf. Facing the canal turn left across road and follow canal towpath, switching to south bank at second road bridge. After about two miles, this circular walk joins the linear walks (just beyond the lock) at Tyle Mill Bridge.

❹ From Tyle Mill Bridge (Grid ref: 627692)

For all four walks, turn away from Tyle Mill Bridge to go south along road, then at end of property 'Rose Court' on right, turn right into narrow path and pass over two stiles. Continue along bottom edge of field with fence on right and after the stile ahead, keep straight on near bottom end of next two fields. After further stile turn half-left up through middle of field to the tallest tree on

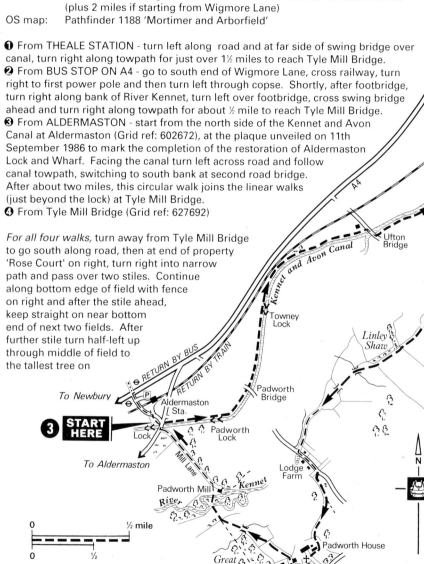

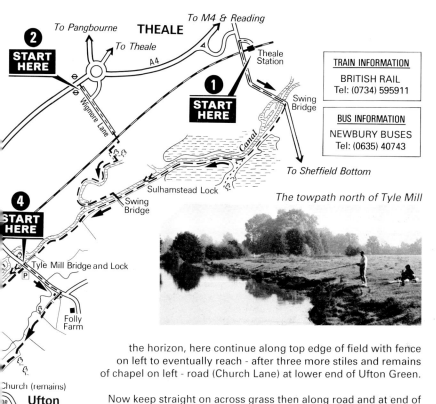

To Pangbourne

THEALE

To M4 & Reading

**②
START
HERE**

To Theale

A4

Theale
Station

Wigmore Lane

**①
START
HERE**

Swing
Bridge

Canal

TRAIN INFORMATION
BRITISH RAIL
Tel: (0734) 595911

BUS INFORMATION
NEWBURY BUSES
Tel: (0635) 40743

To Sheffield Bottom

Sulhamstead Lock

The towpath north of Tyle Mill

**④
START
HERE**

Swing
Bridge

Tyle Mill Bridge and Lock

P

Folly
Farm

Church (remains)

**Ufton
Green**

the horizon, here continue along top edge of field with fence on left to eventually reach - after three more stiles and remains of chapel on left - road (Church Lane) at lower end of Ufton Green.

Now keep straight on across grass then along road and at end of the first field on right, turn right over stile. Follow short fence on right and maintain same direction through middle of field to stile at right-hand end of field boundary ahead, here continue in next two fields with fence on right. At end of copse (Linley Shaw), bear right down wide track round bottom edge of field, then after stile and footbridge in corner, maintain same direction through middle of next field to opening in middle of field boundary ahead. In far corner of following field, at end of fence on right, enter hedged track after stile to follow ditch on right and to reach road here turn left along road. After bungalow on right, pass over stile on right and follow field edge with a fence on right, slowly climbing up towards Padworth House (rebuilt 1769).

Just before house, pass through metal swing gate, then follow path (to left of the buildings) curving right, to enter churchyard of St John the Baptist ahead. Leaving by lych-gate turn sharp right for 60 yards to continue down gravel track, shortly turning left, then right, round barn on right. After stile just ahead, keep down edge of field to further stile at end of fence on right, here bear slightly left through middle of next field to footbridge in far corner. Continue ahead through the middle of two more fields and after crossing weirs to Padworth Mill on right, enter narrow fenced path. Shortly bear left along gravel track (Mill Lane) and at end of this, cross canal. To reach Aldermaston Station and Bus Stop on A4 continue to left along minor road over railway. To return to Tyle Mill Bridge, Wigmore Lane or Theale Station follow the canal bank - see map.

DATE WALKED ☐ 19

Roman Amphitheatre and Foudry Brook

This circular walk is through very pleasant undulating farmland south of Mortimer with extensive views over Hampshire, visiting the impressive 1st century Roman amphitheatre remains at Silchester.

Distance: 5 miles
OS map: Pathfinder 1188 'Mortimer and Arborfield'
Start: Parking area fronting St John the Evangelist, Mortimer (Grid ref: 654646)

Facing church, turn right along West End Road, then take first left into unmade road (St Johns Road) and after about 40 yards turn right into another hedged unmade road. At far end of the road, turn right along tarmac road, Drury Lane, and shortly at junction, turn left along Turks Lane to soon cross county boundary into Hampshire. (Notice bench mark.) Where road forks, keep right along Simms Farm Lane and at end of tarmac, continue straight on along gravel drive to pass between the buildings of Simms Farm. Continue down sunken lane ahead, keep right at bottom, then after metal field gate at bridge over stream (West End Brook), bear slightly left through middle of small field to enter, after footbridge over ditch, woodland ahead - Nine Acre Copse.

Climb up narrow path, then after stile into young plantation, follow ditch on left and after stile in fence on far side, bear left through middle of field. After about 100 yards notice midfield crossing path (reinstated after pressure by the RA) and continue ahead to cross stile on far side. Bear right down increasingly sloping field to pass over footbridge and stile into next field. Now bear left uphill to reach stile on far side, turning right into sunken track which soon leads to corner of road, with entrance gate to Roman amphitheatre close-by on right. Silchester's 12th century church of St Mary, the timber-framed manor house and the incredible Roman town walls are just a few yards ahead. Now retrace

your steps staying on sunken track. On reaching road (Pitfield Lane) keep straight on down road and after Brocas Lands Farm, fork right. Ahead in the distance is seen the spire of St Marys Church, Stratfield Mortimer. Just after Tanhouse Cottages on left and immediately beyond bridge over stream, turn right into hedged path to reach stile and follow edge of field with stream on right. At end of field turn left in front of stile to follow, below on right, Foudry Brook.

Enter next long riverside meadow by footbridge and stile, and after using high stile to pass to left of copse ahead, continue along edge of field with brook on right. About half way along second field, at narrow footbridge over brook, turn left up through middle of field to reach road (Pitfield Lane) after stile, here turn right along road. At junction, turn left up road (The Street) and shortly at bend in road, immediately after property 'Alvernia', turn right down gravel drive.

After stile at end, continue up edge of field with ditch on left and when over stile at top, keep left with hedge on left to reach a further stile, here follow edge of field ahead with metal railings on left. In far corner of field turn right for about 50 yards, then turn left over stile to follow edge of field with fence and trees on left. Shortly at stile ahead, continue in next field on fenced path with trees now on right. Enter copse ahead and after about 60 yards, fork left to reach road. Here move about 15 yards to right to enter through metal swing gate, recreation ground 'The Fairground' opposite. Now go half left across grass, passing through another metal swing gate and to right of tennis courts, to return to church at start.

DATE WALKED ⬚ ⬚ 19

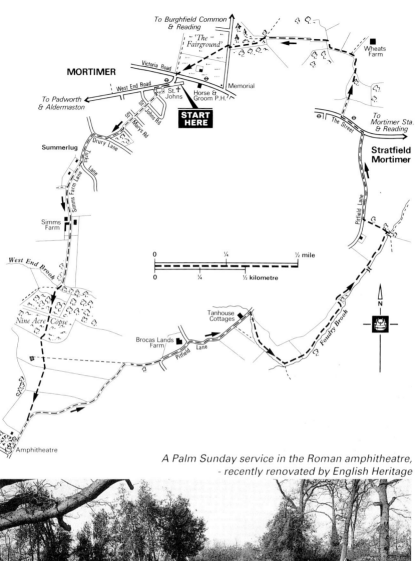

To Burghfield Common
& Reading

"The Fairground"

Wheats Farm

MORTIMER

Victoria Road

Memorial

West End Road

St. Johns

Horse & Groom P.H.

To Padworth
& Aldermaston

START HERE

The Street

To Mortimer Sta.
& Reading

St Johns Rd

St Marys Rd

Drury Lane

Summerlug

Stratfield Mortimer

Turks Lane

Simms Farm Lane

Pitfield Lane

Simms Farm

West End Brook

Nine Acre Copse

Tanhouse Cottages

Foudry Brook

Brocas Lands Farm

Pitfield Lane

0   ¼   ½ mile

0   ¼   ½ kilometre

N

Amphitheatre

A Palm Sunday service in the Roman amphitheatre,
- recently renovated by English Heritage

Grazeley Church and Hopkiln Farm

Ramble 14

This flat circular walk, immediately to the south west of Reading, is across open farmland and along quiet country lanes around Grazeley.

Distance:	3¾ miles
OS Map:	Pathfinder 1188 'Mortimer and Arborfield'
Start:	Fullers Lane, off Grazeley Green Road (Grid ref: 688676). Limited verge parking.

With verge on left, continue along the winding Fullers Lane past Grazeley Manor Farm on left, pass under railway and about 200 yards after bridge, opposite Poundgreen Farm, turn right into Pump Lane. About 80 yards after drive to Hawthorn Cottages on right, turn left over footbridge and through middle of fields with ditch on left and Lambwoodhill Common on right. At waymark post, keep straight on, moving away from ditch on left, to stile in middle of far boundary. Maintain same direction through playing field ahead and after passing through metal swing gate at road, turn left for about 5 yards, then turn left through barrier and along the edge of recreation ground towards the small flint-faced Holy Trinity Church, Grazeley.

At narrow lane ahead, pass through white wooden swing gate opposite and keeping to right-hand side of churchyard, leave by hedged path, then bear very slightly right through middle of field in direction of left-hand end of distant Gravelley Bridge Farm. At end of field, cross footbridge and road (Grazeley Green Road) into fenced path opposite* by stile, then continue ahead along broad hedged farm track. Soon after stile next to gate, track curves slightly left into narrow field. Follow ditch on right and after two ponds nearby on left, go through gateway in corner into next field and continue straight on along edge of three fields with hedge or fence now on left. At end of third field, pass through gateway to reach narrow lane at Hopkiln Farm.

Now turn right along lane (Kybes Lane), follow this through left-hand bend to have Foudry Brook on right, then just before road junction ahead, turn left through gateway along edge of field with wire mesh fence on left - the tall buildings of Reading can just be seen in the distance on right. At corner of field continue ahead through gap in hedge to pass asbestos building on right, then bear slightly right over air-strip to cross ditch and bank to right of kink in far field boundary. About 20 yards into next field, turn right over footbridge. Despite the proximity of Reading and the motorway it is sometimes possible to catch a glimpse of roe-deer or a heron here. Now turn left along edge of field for a few yards to first tree, then bear right across middle of field to distant pylon.

With care cross railway (Reading - Basingstoke line) ahead using stiles on either side, then continue along edge of next field with fence on right - below on right is the course of the old railway line connecting to factory ahead. In next field continue with fence on right and at far end follow it through left-hand for about 50 yards, then pass over stile and footbridge on right to reach road ahead - the heavily fenced establishment on the right is the Royal Ordnance Factory, Burghfield. Now keep left along road (Burnthouse Lane), using verge on right, then at white railing bridge (Burnthouse Bridge) over brook bear left along Fullers Lane to return to parking place at start.

This path has recently been unofficially moved. In this location (where there was previously a ditch) it is often flooded. The Highway Authority is responsible for receiving complaints and taking the appropriate action.

DATE WALKED   19

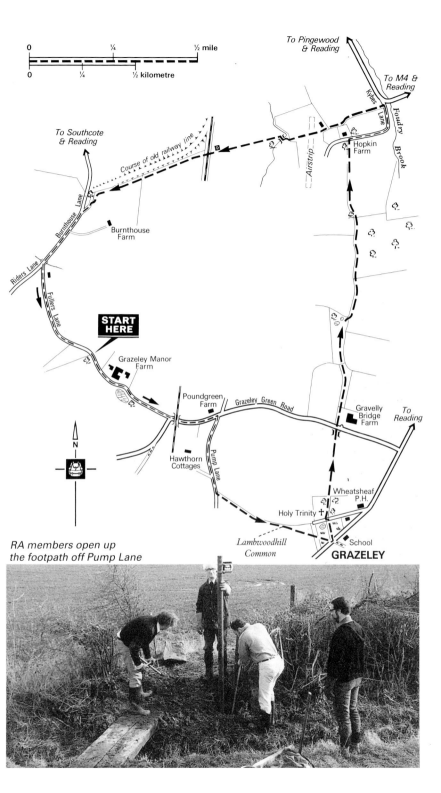

0 ¼ ½ mile

0 ¼ ½ kilometre

To Pingewood & Reading

To M4 & Reading

Kytes Lane

Foudry Brook

To Southcote & Reading

Course of old railway line

Hopkin Farm

Burnthouse Lane

Burnthouse Farm

Riders Lane

Airstrip

Fullers Lane

START HERE

Grazeley Manor Farm

Poundgreen Farm

Grazeley Green Road

Gravelly Bridge Farm

To Reading

N

Hawthorn Cottages

Pump Lane

Wheatsheaf P.H.

Holy Trinity †

School

Lambwoodhill Common

GRAZELEY

RA members open up the footpath off Pump Lane

Devil's Highway
and Beech Hill

Ramble 15

This circular walk passes through pleasant undulating countryside to south and east of Stratfield Mortimer; about one quarter of the route follows the ancient Devil's Highway, which can be very muddy, so do go suitably shod.

Distance: 5¾ miles
OS map: Pathfinder 1188 'Mortimer and Arborfield'
Start: Lay-by just NE of Stratfield Mortimer (Grid ref: 676646)

From lay-by, with care continue along road towards Stratfield Mortimer, then immediately after entrance to sewage works, turn right up edge of two fields with hedge on right. At end of second field pass to left of red brick Wern Cottage to emerge at road, Mortimer Lane, here turn left along road. At road junction ahead, with great care cross to footway opposite and turn left, then after about 50 yards turn right into gravel track past the impressive tall stone church of St Mary's on right. After small brick bridge at entrance to Ladyfield House, enter field just ahead at stile and turn right along raised field-edge path with hedge at first on right and then bank of Foudry Brook.

At end of second field and after stile at footbridge, turn half-left through middle of field to pass through tunnel under railway. After stile on far side follow cross-field path to wooden power-line pole at bend in field boundary (the official line of path passes to right of large mid-field tree and pond). Ignore stile in fence here and continue with hedge on left into narrow part of same field. After stile next to wooden gate, continue on hedged track to eventually reach road after stile next to metal gate, here turn right along road. At junction just after Butlers Lands Farm, turn left into broad hedged track - The Devil's Highway - the Roman Road from London to Silchester.

Follow this ancient highway for about 1½ miles (coincident with the County boundary) and on reaching solitary red brick cottage, turn left along road. About 100 yards after white railed bridge over stream at bend in road, turn right into gently climbing hedged grass track - Donkey Pound Lane. Continue on gravel drive to reach road ahead, here turn left to continue walk, but turn right for about 30 yards to visit the water reservoir given to the inhabitants of Beech Hill on 22nd June 1897 to commemorate "sixty glorious years" reign of Queen Victoria.

Retracing your steps, continue along road for about 60 yards, then turn right up fenced path between cottages and after stile ahead, keep straight on through middle of field. After stile in far boundary maintain same direction through middle of next field to cross stile at metal rails by bridge over ditch, here still keep straight on up through middle of further field to near corner of woodland on horizon. After wooden swing gate in corner of field, keep along edge of two fields with woodland (Little Copse) and then fence on right.

Cross stile ahead in corner of second field, follow wire fence on right and then maintain this direction through middle of field to right-hand end of large tiled barn among the buildings of Great Park Farm. The large house in the distance on right, is Wokefield Park, originally built for a member of the Palmer family in about 1910. After two stiles into small field, pass to left of smaller tiled barn. After further stile, turn left along concrete road through middle of farm buildings. Follow farm road through right-hand bend, then where this road turns left at pair of red brick cottages, continue straight on into field ahead and keeping 20 yards to right of near pylon, maintain same direction over brow of hill. With great care cross railway using stiles on either side and after bridge over Foudry Brook just ahead, turn left to return to parking place at start.

DATE WALKED   19

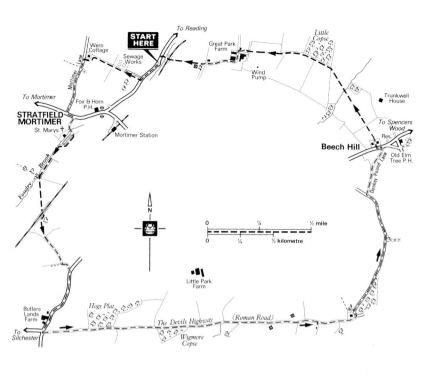

START HERE

To Reading

Great Park Farm

Little Copse

Wern Cottage

Sewage Works

Mortimer Lane

To Mortimer

Wind Pump

Trunkwell House

Fox & Horn P.H.

STRATFIELD MORTIMER

St. Marys †

Mortimer Station

To Spencers Wood

Res.

Beech Hill

Old Elm Tree P.H.

Foudry Brook

N

0   ¼   ½ mile

0   ¼   ½ kilometre

Danley Pound Lane

Butlers Lands Farm

Hogs Plat

Little Park Farm

The Devils Highway   (Roman Road)

To Silchester

Wigmore Copse

Passing through Great Park Farm

Shinfield and Three Mile Cross

This mainly flat circular walk, immediately to the south of Reading, is through the pastures and arable land between Shinfield and Three Mile Cross.

Distance: 4¾ miles
OS Map: Pathfinder 1188 'Mortimer and Arborfield'
Start: Free car park Shinfield village green (Grid ref: 733678)

From car park take main path starting some 25 yards to left of Shinfield House, towards stile in hedgerow. Do not climb stile but turn right into hedged and fenced path with stileway. With care cross main road (A327) ahead, turn left for about 25 yards and turn right into Fairmead Road, then at end turn left along unmade road (Oatlands Road). Immediately after property No. 40, turn right into hedged path and after footbridge bear left into narrower fenced path with fields on right, then at road ahead (Cutbush Lane) turn left along road. At end of field on right, turn left into Leyland Gardens and shortly, at end of garden to chalet bungalow on right, turn right into narrow fenced path, then at main road (A327) ahead, with care cross over using steps on both sides. Continue on tree-lined path through two wooden swing gates, turn left along tarmac footway for about 30 yards to green telephone box, then turn right into road between the buildings of, until recently, the National Food Research Institute.

Follow road through left-hand bend and shortly at wooden swing gate in corner on right, enter and pass through the churchyard of the attractive brick and flint-faced parish church of 'St Mary's' (built 1170). At road (Church Lane) turn right for about 40 yards, then turn left into fenced path and immediately after barrier at end, turn right along concrete road between buildings continuing as fenced path through fields. At end of field on right, turn right over stile with fence on right, to shortly continue down through middle of field and at far side, turn left along field edge with ditch on right.

Just before power line pole, turn right over stile, cross end of narrow field and after further stile, continue on short grass path to reach road (Church Lane). Now turn right along road for about 40 yards then turn left over stile along edge of two sides of field with hedge on left and after stile in corner, continue in next field with hedge on left. After stile and footbridge at end of field, keep straight on with fence on right - here observe to right across motorway, the Shire Hall (completed 1980) on rising ground at Shinfield Park. At edge of M4, turn left over stile and along edge of field with fence on right, then shortly after stile ahead, bear slightly left along edge of next field with hedge nearby on left. After stile at far end of field, turn left into the old A33 and shortly in front of first house on left, 'Milestone Cottage', note old milestone 'Southampton 43' etc.. At end of cul-de-sac, keep straight on along main road (A33) through Three Mile Cross.

About 100 yards after Church Lane, turn left into broad hedged path and after stile follow edge of field with hedge on right, then after further stile continue along edge of next three fields with hedge now on left. Half way along third field, enter fenced path over stile and after next stile, turn left past red brick pavilion on left to follow gravel track curving right. At road ahead (Ryeish Lane) turn left along narrow winding lane and at road junction ahead, keep straight on into fenced path between fields. Ignore footpath on right and at concrete farm road ahead, bear right over stile into broad fenced grass path. Reaching open area, still follow hedge on left to complete the circuit, soon turning right towards buildings at start.

DATE WALKED   ☐   19☐

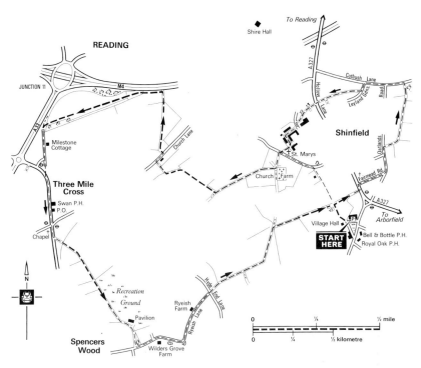

READING

JUNCTION 11

M4

A33

To Reading

Shire Hall

Cotbush Lane

A327

Hollin Lane

Leyland Gdns

Shinfield

Oatlands

Road

Church Lane

St. Marys

Church Farm

Farmead Rd.

A327

To Arborfield

Milestone Cottage

Three Mile Cross

Swan P.H.
P.O.

Chapel

Village Hall

START HERE

Bell & Bottle P.H.

Royal Oak P.H.

N

Recreation Ground

Pavilion

Ryeish Farm

Hyde End Lane

Ryeish Lane

Spencers Wood

Wilders Grove Farm

0   ¼   ½ mile
0   ¼   ½ kilometre

A helping hand - part of the fun, on a local walk with all the family

Blackwater River and Swallowfield Park

Ramble 17

This circular walk is through the pleasant gently undulating farmland to the south and east of Swallowfield, with a brief but pleasing visit to the Blackwater River.

Distance: 6¾ miles
OS map: Pathfinder 1188 'Mortimer and Arborfield'
Start: Limited verge parking junction of Trowes Lane and Charlton Lane, Swallowfield (Grid ref: 724643)

Facing south, from road junction continue along Trowes Lane for about 40 yards then turn left into tarmac drive and immediately before this turns right, enter narrow fenced path with hedge on right. Near end of drive, turn right, through gap in hedge and over footbridge. Continue slightly left through middle of field towards highest point of barn ahead to reach Trowes Lane again, here turn left along road. At junction ahead, turn right along road for about 40 yards, then turn left over two stiles at either end of farm building. Following hedge on left, maintain this direction through middle of field to meet and follow hedge on left again, then after stile in corner turn left along narrow road - the Berks/Hants County boundary and the Devil's Highway (the Roman road from London to Silchester).

At cross-roads, turn right along road, then eventually where this turns right at Riseley Mill, keep straight on along gravel track. Shortly at end of wood on right, turn half-left through wooden gate to soon cross wooden footbridge over River Whitewater. On far side, bear right through wooden swing gate into fenced path and after metal swing gate ahead, continue along edge of field with hedge on right. At end of field cross over road and after a further 10 yards ahead, turn left into gravel track parallel with road, along edge of Bramshill Plantation. When Cordery's Farm appears on left, follow track through right-hand bend to eventually re-join Well House Lane, here

turn left along road for about 40 yards, then turn right along edge of field with ditch and trees on right. At end of field, turn left along bank of Blackwater River.

At end of field curve away from river to reach road after stile, here turn right towards a ford, then turn left over stile shortly to continue along river bank. At footbridge ahead, cross river to continue on far bank, cutting the corner at first bend. At gate ahead, turn right over stile and up fenced path around two sides of field to reach road (Nutbeam Lane) after stile and footbridge, here turn right along road. At road junction keep left and immediately after red brick house (Sandpit Farm), turn left into short broad hedged grass track and after stile next to wooden gate, keep straight on through middle of field to double stile at gap in hedge on horizon. In next field turn right along edge of field with fence on right for about 100 yards to top of rise (Chill Hill) - here pause for distant views of Reading. Now turn left down through middle of field following row of four well spaced oak trees and after two stiles close together at bottom, turn right along hedged track (Raggetts Lane). At road ahead turn left and shortly at junction, bear right into broad hedged track curving left to reach road (Reeds Lane), here with care turn right up road. At start of right-hand bend in road, turn left over stile and along edge of field with hedge on left, to enter Swallowfield Park.

After next stile, continue along field track with hedge on left. LOOK OUT for metal field gate on left, where pass into adjacent field and continue in same direction, now with ditch on right. Cross next stile and follow field edge, finally turning left, with All Saints Church (built 1256) nearby on right, to reach stile at road. Turn left along road and shortly, at start of bend, turn right over the narrow concrete and metal Salter's Bridge into narrow hedged path and after further footbridge over The Broadwater, keep straight on through middle of field. After

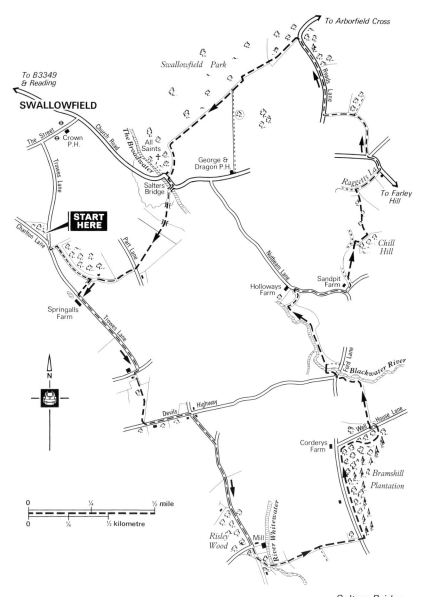

To Arborfield Cross

Swallowfield Park

To B3349
& Reading

SWALLOWFIELD

The Street

Crown
P.H.

Church Road

The Broadwater

All
Saints

George &
Dragon P.H.

Salters
Bridge

Raggetts La.

To Farley
Hill

Trowes Lane

Charlton Lane

**START
HERE**

Part Lane

Springalls
Farm

Trowes Lane

Devils

Highway

Risley
Wood

Mill

River Whitewater

Nutbean Lane

Holloways
Farm

Sandpit
Farm

Chill
Hill

Ford Lane

Blackwater River

Corderys
Farm

Well House Lane

*Bramshill
Plantation*

Reads Lane

N

0   ¼   ½ mile

0   ¼   ½ kilometre

stile and concrete bridge, bear slightly
right through middle of next field to
reach stile at road (Part Lane). Here
cross road and after stile opposite,
continue along edge of field with ditch
on left. After next stile, still with ditch on
left, enter narrow fenced path passing
bungalow, to retrace your steps to
parking place at start.

DATE WALKED   19

Salters Bridge

Pudding Lane and Farley Hill

This circular walk is through the gently undulating rich farmland between Arborfield Cross and Farley Hill.

Distance: 5¼ miles
OS Map: Pathfinder 1188 'Mortimer and Arborfield'
Start: Small free car park at Arborfield Cross, about 200 yards down Swallowfield Road from 'The Bull' (Grid ref: 760670)

Leaving car park, turn right along road and shortly at end of recreation ground, at barn, turn right into broad hedged track - Pudding Lane. At main road (A327, Reading Road) ahead, turn left along footway, then shortly after second bus-stop on left, turn left into Greensward Lane and immediately after last house on right, turn right through stileway into Pound Copse. Fork left along Permitted Path and at end of copse turn right to cross stile and follow field edge with hedge and trees on left. At end of field, in corner, cross stile and turn left to enter large field and continue ahead with hedge on left.

Go right at end of field with a fence and row of newly planted trees now on left, and after stile next to metal gates continue on broad fenced track. Follow track through right and left-hand bends, with red brick house (Kenneys Farm) on right to eventually reach road (Swallowfield Road), here turn right keeping to verge on right. About 100 yards after Tanners Farm House, turn left across road into broad climbing woodland track (Kiln Hill). At top of climb pass drive to house on right and continue on gravel track for about 40 yards, then turn right into narrow woodland path slowly descending and shortly to follow fence to field on left. At end of woodland, pass through stileway and turn left along broad hedged track - here look left for glimpse of Farley Hall. Continue straight on at road junction up (Bungler's Hill), past Clarkes Farm, keeping where possible to verge on

right, then about 50 yards after Sandpit Lane on right, fork left on tarmac drive continuing as path, to shortly reach on right the small red brick church of St John the Evangelist, Farley Hill.

Continue with wooden fence on right, turn left at road ahead keeping to verge and about 100 yards after bend in road, turn right into narrow road (Church Lane). At end of Cricket Club ground, turn left into fenced path and at road ahead turn right along road. Just beyond pair of red brick houses on left, fork left into field and slowly moving away from hedge on left make for large oak tree about 30 yards to right of corner, then keep along edge of next field with hedge on left. On far side of field turn left into broad hedged track.

At junction of tracks ahead, turn left along woodland path (Wokingham Lane) for nearly 100 yards, then turn right up bank and along edge of field with hedge on left. At woodland ahead, bear right up bank and continue along winding field edge to enter woodland ahead in field corner. Emerging by stile at far side, keep straight on through middle of field to stile at right-hand end of conifers on horizon. Continue on fenced path with high hedge to Arborfield Court on left and after next stile bear slightly left down through middle of field to another stile in far left-hand corner. Turn left and after small footbridge and stile, keep down edge of field with houses on right and shortly after further stile, turn right along road to return to car park at start.

DATE WALKED 25 | 08 | 19 2008

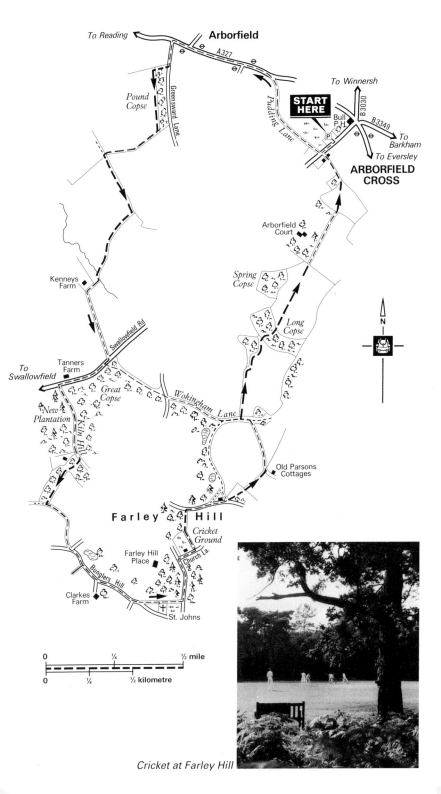

To Reading

Arborfield

A327

Pound Copse

Greensward Lane

Pudding Lane

START HERE

Bull P.H.

P

To Winnersh

B 3030

B 3349

To Barkham

To Eversley

ARBORFIELD CROSS

Arborfield Court

Spring Copse

Long Copse

N

Kenneys Farm

Swallowfield Rd

To Swallowfield

Tanners Farm

Great Copse

New Plantation

Kiln Hill

Wokingham Lane

Old Parsons Cottages

Farley Hill

Cricket Ground

Bunglers Hill

Farley Hill Place

Church La.

Clarkes Farm

St. Johns

0	¼	½ mile

0	¼	½ kilometre

Cricket at Farley Hill

Fleet Copse and Rectory Farm

This circular walk provides some fine views over the gently rolling countryside around Finchampstead and includes some water meadows adjacent to the Blackwater River. The optional extension around Longmoor Lake at the California Country Park increases the distance to 5½ miles.

Distance: 5 or 5½ miles
OS Map: Pathfinder 1188 'Mortimer and Arborfield'
Start: Wokingham District Council's California Country Park (Grid ref: 785650)

From car park, return to entrance to Country Park and turn right along road, keeping to footway on right, then at property No. 63A 'The Cuckoos' turn sharp left across road and follow wide unsurfaced track to enter narrow grassy path between timber-clad stable block on left and fenced compound. After stile ahead, continue straight on along broad fenced path up edge of field. Along here look half-left to see the brick tower of the ancient Finchampstead Church among trees on high ground, visited later on walk. At road ahead (Commonfield Lane) at Beech Cottage, keep straight on over two stiles close together and after third stile just ahead, continue along edge of field with hedge on left. At further stile near top of rise, keep straight on in next field to another stile at path junction, here turn sharp right, between rails, into fenced path with large field on left.

After woodland on right, still continue ahead keeping large trees on left. Cross stile into narrow fenced path passing solitary house on right. Cross narrow tarmac drive, go through wooden swing-gate to follow line of wire fence on right. On far side of field, after two swing-gates turn right along road (B3348) keeping to verge on right, then about halfway down hill, immediately after Fleet Hill Cottage, turn left into broad gravel drive. On reaching buildings of Fleethill Farm on right, keep straight on along edge of two large fields (part of the broad flat valley of the Blackwater River) with Fleet Copse on left.

Just after stile at end of second field, turn left up broad woodland track (Longwater Lane). At start of houses, to continue walk turn left, but first go ahead for about 20 yards to small plaque on left giving details of the history of the area and an incident involving King Henry VII on 6th November 1501. Retracing your steps, follow climbing path with hedge on left and fence on right to reach road (B3348, The Village) after stile, here turn left along road keeping to verge on right. Just after houses on right, turn right up tarmac drive towards Rectory Farm.

At gateway, just before farm buildings, cross stile on right and, at end of field on right turn right up fenced path to reach further stile with footbridge then turn left to follow path around edge of field. At the top, turn left up hedged track to reach, after swing-gate and several steps, on top of a man-made mound, the part-Saxon brick faced Parish Church of St James. Pass to left of church, then bear left down tarmac drive and just before 'The Queen's Oak', turn left along White Horse Lane - the section between the two bends being part of the Devil's Highway - the Roman Road between London and Silchester. At second left-hand bend, fork right through swing-gate into descending fenced and hedged track, then at houses ahead, keep straight on along gravel drive (Warren Lane) and at road ahead (Nine Mile Ride), turn left along footway opposite.

At entrance to Country Park, enter narrow woodland path to the right of, and parallel with, the tarmac drive and after about 150 yards bear right over narrow wooden footbridge (Paul's Bridge). About 10 yards beyond foot-bridge, turn right along raised climbing path curving to the left and after passing through open park with pond on right and fenced area on left, descend into woodland path with Longmoor Lake

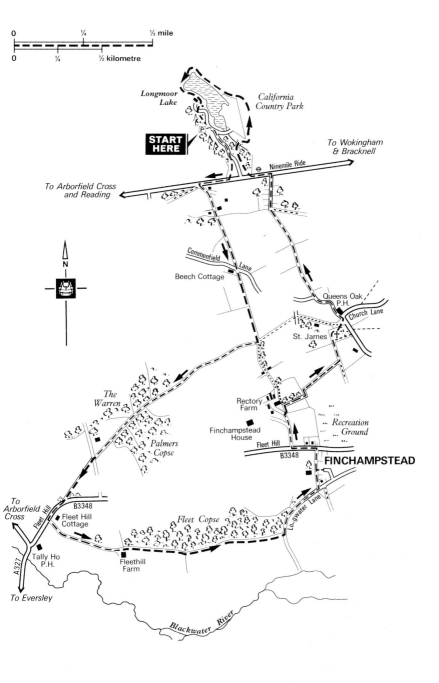

START HERE

Longmoor Lake

California Country Park

To Wokingham & Bracknell

Ninemile Ride

To Arborfield Cross and Reading

Commonfield Lane

Beech Cottage

Queens Oak P.H.

Church Lane

St. James

The Warren

Palmers Copse

Rectory Farm

Finchampstead House

Recreation Ground

Fleet Hill

B3348

FINCHAMPSTEAD

To Arborfield Cross

Fleet Hill

B3348

Fleet Hill Cottage

A327

Tally Ho P.H.

Fleethill Farm

Fleet Copse

Longwater Lane

To Eversley

Blackwater River

N

nearby on left. Continue around edge of lake passing to right of picnic area, then after small green-tiled building on far side of car park, take short woodland path to right of drive to return to overflow car park at start.

DATE WALKED   19

Hatch Farm and Loaders Lane

Ramble 20

This short circular walk, to the south-west of Winnersh, is across the fields and along tracks to the west of Sindlesham.

Distance: 2½ miles
OS Map: Pathfinder 1188 'Mortimer and Arborfield'
Start: Car Park on west side of Bearwood Recreation Ground, Sindlesham (Grid ref: 776698). Alternatively there is parking space in Mill Lane under M4 bridge.

With your back to car park, with care turn left along Mole Road (B3030) and shortly at junction, turn right into winding Mill Lane keeping to footway on right. About 40 yards after the buildings to Hatch Farm on left, pass over stile on left and follow edge of two fields with fence and, shortly, M4 motorway on your right. After footbridge, steps and stile, keep straight on along edge of next field with fence and M4 still on right. About half-way along length of field, at signpost, turn half left through middle of field to stile under large oak tree, here continue in next field with fence on right. After about 50 yards, turn right over stile and footbridge, and keep along top edge of this small field. In far corner of field, turn left over stile next to gate, to shortly reach bend in track ahead, here keep right along track - Loaders Lane.

Entering woodland ahead, keep straight on to end of buildings on right, then turn left along broad gravel track - Julkes Lane. At conifer at end of trees on left, turn left up bank and along edge of field with metal railings on left to reach footbridge and stile. In next field continue to end of woodland on left, then go very slightly right through middle of field to stile in far boundary fence. Now keep straight on with fence on right and after two stiles and footbridge at far end, turn right along gravel track.

Shortly, at junction of tracks, fork left past cottages on left along (Gypsy Lane) which soon becomes a hedged soil track. After Melton Cottage on right, continue on gravel surface, then when this track turns right, keep straight on into narrow path between ditch on left and fence to golf driving range on right. After sleeper footbridge ahead, bear right around two sides of woodland area to reach gravel drive at road, here with care cross road to footway opposite and turn right to return to car park at start.

DATE WALKED | | 19

The changing countryside; 1883 and 1913 OS map extracts (Reading Reference Library)

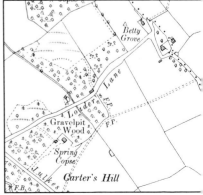

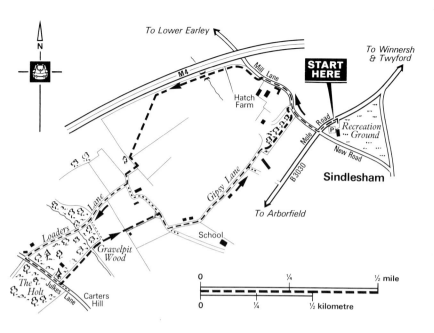

Publications

Each illustrated booklet contains twenty or more short circular walks.

Rambling for Pleasure in East Berkshire (1st series) £1.20
Rambling for Pleasure in East Berkshire (2nd series)..£1.20
Rambling for Pleasure Around Reading (1st series)..£1.75
Rambling for Pleasure Around Reading (2nd series) £1.75
Rambling for Pleasure Along the Thames (full colour) £2.50
Kennet Valley & Watership Down (full colour)...£2.50
The Three Castles Path (Long Distance Path)...£2.50
Footpath Map:
Windsor and The Great Park (Two colour A3 size) 50p

All these publications, including this booklet, are available from local bookshops and
stationers or by post 40p extra (cheques payable to East Berk RA Group) from:
Pat Hayers, 16 Lanterns Walk, Farthingales, Maidenhead, Berkshire SL6 1TG

Theale Lake and Whitehouse Green

A varied walk through fields, along lakeside and canal bank, within the still mainly rural parish of Burghfield. Easily accessible by bus if preferred from the fringes of Reading at Calcot, or starting from Burghfield village.

Distance: about 5¼ to 6 miles
OS Map: Pathfinder 1172 'Reading';
                      1188 'Mortimer & Arborfield'
Start: either CALCOT, Reading -
                      bus-stop by Beansheaf
                      Stores, Charrington Road
                      (route 25) (Grid ref: 663716)
                      or BURGHFIELD village
                      green, hard-standing at
                      roadside (Grid ref: 666685)
                      see paragraph 4 below.

From bus-stop take narrow tree-lined path behind Beansheaf Stores leading to open parkland. Here bear right to join gravel path over wide culvert (ditch), soon to cross wooden footbridge and turn right along bank of Holy Brook. At end of meadow turn left over two stiles with railway between. Go ahead through meadow to cross stile and River Kennet at Hissey's Bridge. Immediately after bridge turn right down path, with river close-by on right. Where path devides, take right fork, still following stream. Pass under M4 and immediately turn left.

After 75 yards bear left to cross wooden footbridge and go straight on along wide track, now with open views across Theale Lake - a popular sailing venue. At end of lake, facing double metal gates (quarry entrance) bear left into narrow fenced path.

At end of this path turn right over wooden footbridge and second (metal) bridge, then straight over gravel area and a third bridge, before turning right along bank of deep ditch (Clayhill Brook) leading to stile at road. Cross road and turn left along verge for 40 yards, then turn right down steps and over stile, now to follow left side of two fields ahead, leading to Green Farm. Take track on

left of buildings and continue along roadway. If returning to Burghfield village, take cross-field path on left, by Victorian farmhouse, through two fields to reach School Lane. To continue the circular walk look for gap into first field on right after farmhouse and skip the next paragraph.

FROM BURGHFIELD, starting on north side of hedged triangular green and with back to 'Six Bells', follow right-hand footway and bear right at crossroads. At end of houses on left, turn right into School Lane and where tarmac ends turn left over stile, along cross-field path bearing half-right and passing mid-field power-line pole to stile at gap in hedge. Here turn half-left across next field to a point just left of single tree. Cross lane ahead via gaps in hedges as we join the route from Calcot.

For both routes, bear slightly left across field, passing right of water-trough. Cross sleeper-bridge over ditch and turn right, following field-edge path with splendid row of oaks as your guide. At top of rise, bear right out of field, into enclosed path, soon to reach and turn left along lane (Bennett's Hill). Where lane turns right, bear left into field entrance and follow field-edge with trees on right. Cross plank-bridge in corner and go straight on to find sleeper-bridge at road (Theale Road).

Cross road and turn right along footway. At end of houses continue on verge and take first turning left (Folly Lane). Follow this quiet lane and at sharp left bend (Whitehouse Green) bear right into brick-flanked gateway and immediately turn left along boundary of 'Barnyards' (a recently diverted right of way). After about 70 yards turn left through archway in hedge and then right, along broad strip leading to stile. Take cross-field path ahead, passing left of pylon and at bottom corner continue down track to road junction. Now turn right and where road forks bear left. Follow lane (or grassy strip along lakeside) and where lane turns left, turn right into Lower Kennet Water Park, along winding woodland path, soon to cross low bank on left. Continue between stream on left and lake on right, shortly to reach towpath of Kennet and Avon Canal.

The canal section between Newbury and Reading, known as the Kennet Navigation, is also the oldest of the three parts which make up the 'K & A', having opened in 1723. Along its 18½ miles, 20 locks were built to retain the water as it fell 134 feet between the two towns.

Turn right along canal bank for a little over a mile, passing Theale swing-bridge, Sheffield and Garston locks. Shortly after Garston Lock, where path divides, bear left following canal to reach M4 bridge. Walkers starting from Calcot retrace their steps from here via Hissey's Bridge and railway crossing. Those starting from Burghfield turn right in front of M4 bridge and follow path towards Theale Lake (see paragraph 2).

DATE WALKED [|] 19

Theale Lake

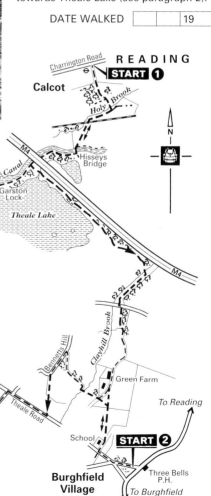

Milkmaids Bridge and the Holy Brook

This easy stroll starts but a stone's throw from the centre of Reading. The low-lying Kennet River meadows have kept the builders at bay leaving an area of almost hidden countryside on the town's doorstep, known mainly to fishermen and local wildlife.

Distance: 4 miles
OS Map: Pathfinder 1172 'Reading'
Start: Bus-stop on bridge in Berkeley Avenue just W of Elgar Road traffic lights* (Grid ref: 714726). Easy access by bus on routes 24 & 44/45.

NOTE: Motorists can start from Reading Link Retail Park in Rose Kiln Lane - see map - beginning walk at LAST paragraph.

From lay-by at bus-stop in Berkeley Avenue cross road turning right and within a few yards turn left down iron-railed steps to bank of Kennet River and turn right along towpath. This part of the river forms a section of the Kennet and Avon Canal, opened in 1723, spanning the 18½ miles between Reading and Newbury. Parts of the canal follow the original course of the river while some stretches were specially constructed, to carry the 20,000 tons of goods being transported annually by the end of the 18th century.

After nearly a mile along the towpath, pass under new bridge (and admire the detailed brickwork). Overhead is Rose Kiln Lane - a name recalling a brickworks once nearby. Shortly ahead on left notice Foudry Brook joining the Kennet. On right we pass the distinctive modern Thames Water control building in Fobney Meadow, a design in metal and glass by prominent architect Nicholas Grimshaw. Reaching old pumping station buildings turn left over bridge and then right, to pass Fobney Lock, and continue along broad track, now on left bank of canal.

Here the Kennet has parted company with the canal for a stretch but soon reunites where the path goes over an unusual 'labyrinth' weir, to turn right at stile. Soon pass under railway arch, continuing along riverbank to reach and turn right over concrete footbridge. Follow this path to view the pleasantly situated Southcot Lock. The Victorians built a pumping station here in 1850 to

Brookmill Bridge

provide a much needed fresh water supply for the fast growing population of Reading. From lock walk back a few yards and cross iron-railed footbridge (Milkmaids Bridge), then bear right along drive, tarmac at first.

Go under railway, turn right and follow path at foot of embankment. Then turn right again under railway and immediately left, up narrow rising path, soon between railings. Cross footbridge over dismantled railway to emerge at Wensley Road. Turn left and shortly, at bend in road, left again, up tarmac path to follow enclosed track leading to road by entrance lodges (Coley Park). Now go straight on, through swing-gate, to reach Wensley Road again. Here turn right and shortly cross over to bear left into The Old Lane. On reaching road junction bear right along Brookmill.

Just beyond Brookmill go ahead over bridge of Holy Brook. (By turning RIGHT here, a delightful detour is possible along this unspoilt river scenery - see map.) To continue our circuit, however, turn left over bridge and follow bank with stream on left. After two stiles

continue on gravel path with the 'hanging gardens of Coley', as they might be called, on opposite bank.

At end of car park cross stream over broad footbridge, left again for a few yards, then turn right, across courtyard leading to footway through attractive modern development, Admirals Court. Reaching Rose Kiln Lane continue ahead, turning right at traffic lights, back into Berkeley Avenue.

Reputed to be the only crossing point in the country where a road meets a street, a lane and an avenue. Not a lot of people know that!

DATE WALKED [   ][19]

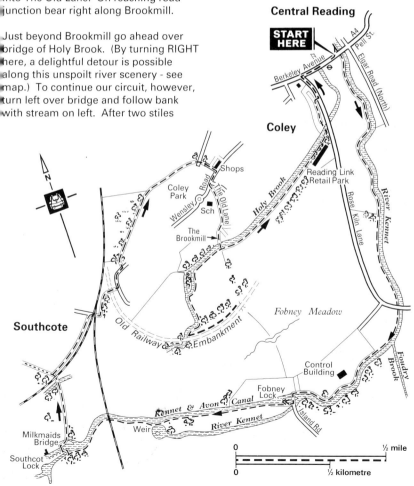

Bramshill Plantation and New Mill Ford

This walk includes an interesting variety of scenery; old parkland around Farley Hill; riverside meadows of the Blackwater Valley; Forestry Commission landscaping at Bramshill Plantation. Some of the paths can be very muddy so do go suitable shod.

Distance:	6 miles
OS Map:	Pathfinder 1188 'Mortimer and Arborfield'
Start:	Entrance to King George's Field, Castle Road, Farley Hill (Grid ref: 752644)

With back to King George's Field, go left along road for 50 yards and turn left into track, to pass church and bowling club. At road continue for 40 yards then cross over to enter narrow Sandpit Lane.

Shortly after Dacre Farm, bear left into wide gravel track with woodland on left at first, followed by parkland of Farley Court. At far end of bridleway turn right along lane and shortly left over footbridge, before gateway to Jouldings Farm. Follow right-hand field edge and after stile in corner go half-right across narrow end of field, and over a pair of stiles into next field, with river nearby on right. Follow wooden fence to far side and cross another pair of stiles beside old metal gates. Keep left of two mid-field trees and after stile at field boundary turn right along hedged path, shortly to cross Blackwater River.

Stile by gate leads into narrow path which twists and turns through Well House Farm to emerge on gravel drive leading to road. Here turn left for about 100 yards before turning right into Bramshill Common Woods. From the entrance take track forking right and shortly right again, along a gorse-lined forest path. Where path twists, continue ahead, now with deep ditch on left. When path reaches exit to road, turn left for 50 paces and then right, in same direction as before. Follow well-used track to road just opposite Cordery's Farm.

At this point, turn left and follow this wide grass strip for about ½ mile (allow, say 10 minutes) and take care to look out for bridleway sign on other side of road (BEFORE Hall's Farm). Cross road into bridleway and follow field-edge with trees on left. At first field opening turn left over ditch, along hedgerow on left and at end of large field cross footbridge and stile. Go ahead across paddock to reach, after another stile, Springwater Farm. Follow tarmac drive ahead to road.

New Mill Ford

Here turn sharp left along road and opposite Yew Tree Cottage turn right over stile to re-enter woodland. After 20 paces turn right through gap, along clear path with occasional painted yellow arrows. Path bends, crosses footbridge and forest 'haul route'. Despite disturbed ground, maintain direction ahead, cross second 'haul route' and follow pebbley track ahead, alongside dense firs on right. At end of pebbles turn left along straight sandy bridleway.

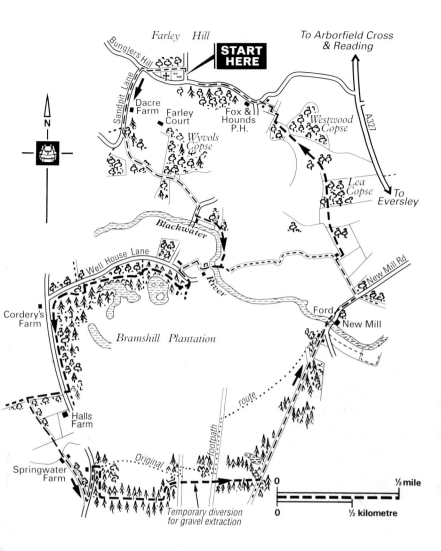

On far side of open common pass pylon (on right) and keep straight on as track continues past properties to lane junction. Here bear left, to cross via long footbridge, the Blackwater at New Mill Ford.

Continue up lane from ford, take first turning left and just before white house turn right at metal gate and along short track. Turn left entering field and follow stiles ahead linking three fields and finally small copse. After footbridge and stile beyond copse, path continues mid-field in same direction, with shallow tree-lined ditch close-by at first.

Eventually this large field narrows to stile in corner. Continue through wooded strip soon to reach and cross stile on right. At end of old iron railings, turn left over stile, now with field on right. Turn right across bottom of lawn and then immediately left on very narrow path between houses to road. Turn left to pass 'Fox & Hounds', along footway back to start.

DATE WALKED   19

Lash Brook and Shiplake Lock

The shorter walk of 2¾ miles includes a justly popular length of unspoilt Thames scenery above Shiplake Lock before climbing the bluff on which stands Shiplake Church. Before long it should be possible to extend the route by a mile using a new link being created by the Countryside Commission as part of the Thames Path, a new National Trail. (Watch local press for details.)

Distance: 2¾ or 3¾ miles
OS Map: Pathfinder 1172 'Reading'
Start: Playing-field car park at Memorial Hall, Memorial Avenue, Shiplake (Grid ref: 764787). If parking several cars, please check beforehand with caretaker - tel: (01734) 403303.

Turn right out of car park and follow splendid rows of maple trees along Memorial Avenue. At Shiplake Cross, with great care cross main road, going 30 yards along Mill Lane before bearing left into unmade, mainly tree-lined, New Road. Go straight on at crossing, soon to reach junction with lane (Mill Road).

FOR THE SHORTER WALK turn right along lane until reaching pillar box on left. Turn left down drive for about 50 yards before turning right over stile. Cross corner of meadow and over stile, turning right along field-edge with fence on right. After two more stiles, turn right along lane (by Mill House), the joining point with the longer walk. Skip the next two paragraphs.

FOR THE LONGER WALK (When it becomes available) cross Mill Road into drive ahead, to left of Virginia Cottage. Pass the quaint Lashbrook Chapel (once a papermill store) and into narrow footpath leading to stile and plank-bridge over Lash Brook. Turn left along field edge and pass under railway viaduct with stiles either side. Then look out half-right for new path across water-meadows ahead to reach riverbank to right of cottage, near site of one-time ferry to Berkshire bank. Here turn right along Thames Path, passing varied properties on far bank, dominated by Wargrave Manor (presently owned by the Sultan of Oman), perched in hilltop

Opposite Philimore's Island